Caves of the Thousand Buddhas
Treasure-House of Chinese Art

Brad Burnham

The Rosen Publishing Group's

PowerKids Press™

New York

For Tung

Published in 2003 by The Rosen Publishing Group, Inc.
29 East 21st Street, New York, NY 10010

First Edition

Editor: Nancy MacDonell Smith
Book Design: Michael J. Caroleo and Michael de Guzman
Layout Design: Colin Dizengoff

Photo Credit: Cover, title page © The Purcell Team/CORBIS; pp. 4, 8, 11–12, 15–16, 20 © Pierre Colombel/CORBIS; pp. 7, 19 © Wolfgang Kaehler/CORBIS.

Burnham, Brad.
Caves of the thousand Buddhas: treasure-house of Chinese art / Brad Burnham. — 1st ed.
p. cm. — (Famous caves of the world)
Includes bibliographical references and index.
  ISBN 0-8239-6260-1
1. Dunhuang Caves (China)—Juvenile literature. 2. Dunhuang Xian (China)—Antiquities—Juvenile literature.
I. Title. II. Series.
  DS793.T79B87 2003
    931—dc21

                                              2001007772

Manufactured in the United States of America

Contents

1 Cave Temples 5

2 The Cliff Face 6

3 Inside the Cave Temples 9

4 Buddhism 10

5 Building the Caves 13

6 Decorating the Caves 14

7 Beautiful Paintings 17

8 In Need of Repair 18

9 The Secret Room 21

10 Today 22

Glossary 23

Index 24

Web Sites 24

Caves of the Thousand Buddhas
Dunhuang, China

CHINA

Cave Temples

About 1,600 years ago, a man named Ts'un Lo wanted to have a place to pray. Ts'un Lo was a follower of **Buddha**. He decided to build a **temple** near the city of Dunhuang, in western China. He found a peaceful place on the banks of the shallow Da River just 12 miles (19 km) away from Dunhuang.

Ts'un Lo did not build a temple on the riverbank using wood or brick. Instead he dug a cave into the cliff that was facing the river and decorated it to look like the inside of a temple. Ts'un Lo's cave temple was not the first of its kind in the world, but it was the first of many to be built at this site. The caves came to be known as the Caves of the Thousand Buddhas.

The Da River Valley is in the province of Kansu sheng, in western China. Hundreds of years ago, this was an important trading center.

The Cliff Face

Today the sides of the cliffs at the Caves of the Thousand Buddhas have more than 450 cave temples in them. The caves are arranged in rows. Each row has several levels of caves, one on top of the other. Some levels have **balconies**. The balconies connect one cave to another. Some of the balconies stick out from the cliff face and are supported by wooden poles. Many of the balconies have **collapsed** over time, but some are still in good shape. There is also a nine-story building that was built into the cliff face about 100 years ago. The building protects a giant, 90-foot-high (27.5-m-high) sculpture of Buddha that was carved out of the cliff face. The building protects the statue from the wind and the rain.

From the outside, the Caves of the Thousand Buddhas look like a large apartment building.

Inside the
Cave Temples

The insides of the caves are covered with decorations from floor to ceiling. The walls are decorated with paintings and statues, and the ceilings are decorated with colorful shapes and patterns. The floors of some caves are covered with clay bricks.

The artwork in the caves shows images of people and images of religious figures. The religious figures are from the religion of **Buddhism**. The main religious figure shown in the caves is Buddha. It's because there are so many images of Buddha in the caves that they have been given the name *Ch'ien Fo Tung*, which means "Caves of the Thousand Buddhas" in Chinese.

This painting is called The Parables of the Sacred Way. *A parable is a short story that illustrates a religious belief or a moral.*

Buddhism

Today millions of people around the world follow the religion of Buddhism. The religion was started more than 2,000 years ago in India by Buddha. Buddha was a man who gave up all his wealth and belongings to become at peace with everything around him.

Buddhists study the teachings of Buddha and **meditate** to find peace and wisdom. Temples are places where Buddhists can pray and meditate. There are many kinds of temples. Some are large buildings. Some are small cave temples, like the ones at the Caves of the Thousand Buddhas. Temples are decorated with images of Buddha, his followers, and peaceful places. The images help Buddhists to find peace and wisdom while they meditate.

Buddha is often shown sitting in meditation, as he is in this statue from the Caves of the Thousand Buddhas.

Building the Caves

The Caves of the Thousand Buddhas are built in a cliff that is made of a rock called conglomerate. This kind of rock is made of small pebbles that are held together by a dry, powdery material. The cave builders at the Caves of the Thousand Buddhas could cut into the rock with simple tools, such as small axes or shovels.

The cave builders made caves that were square or rectangular in shape. The caves range in size from a small closet to a large hall. One of the largest caves measures 40 feet (12.5 m) wide, 70 feet (22 m) long, and 29 feet (9 m) high.

These three statues of bodhisattvas are in a space that was cut into the rock. Bodhisattvas are wise people who help Buddhists to achieve peace and wisdom.

Decorating the Caves

The builders of the caves wanted to paint them to look like the insides of temples. The surfaces of the cave walls were not flat enough to paint on, so the builders put **plaster** on the walls.

The plaster was made from riverbed mud, straw, animal hair, and animal **dung**. After the ingredients were mixed together, the plaster was put on the walls and ceilings in thick layers. When the plaster dried, the walls were smooth and ready for paint.

Plaster was also used to make many of the statues. The center section of a statue was made of straw or rock. Plaster was put on top of the straw or rock and shaped into an image.

Plaster forms a smooth coating for the walls of this cave and for the statues. The iron railing keeps visitors from touching the plaster, which could cause harm.

Beautiful Paintings

The walls of the caves are decorated with beautiful **murals**. Some murals have images of the lives of the people who lived in the area when the caves were built. There are images of farmers and **warriors** in these murals. The murals on the ceilings usually have patterns of shapes and lines that make the ceiling seem very high.

Most of the murals have images of beautiful places. Buddha, musicians, dancers, and animals are in these beautiful scenes. In one cave, there are tigers, monkeys, and a white elephant in the murals. Some of the murals show **mythical** animals, such as gryphons. A gryphon is an imaginary animal that has a lion's body and an eagle's head and wings.

This mural shows warriors wearing armor to protect them as they ride into battle.

In Need of Repair

The Caves of the Thousand Buddhas have been used for more than a thousand years. Unfortunately, they were not always very well taken care of. In the 1890s, a man named Wang Yuanlu visited the caves and saw that the paint was peeling off the murals, some walls had collapsed, and statues had fallen apart. He decided to take care of the caves to prevent further **damage**.

Wang Yuanlu spent many years and much of his money repairing the damaged statues and murals in the caves. He also built the building that covers one of the large statues of Buddha. Other people joined Wang Yuanlu to repair the damage to the caves. Together they formed a **monastery** to look after the Caves of the Thousand Buddhas.

This is one of several giant statues of Buddha that can be seen at the Caves of the Thousand Buddhas. The statue is carved out of the side of the cliff.

The Secret Room

One day Wang Yuanlu noticed that one of the murals was hollow. When he broke through the mural, he found a small room that was full of paintings and written materials. These items had been put in the room more than 800 years earlier for safekeeping. They were very important **artifacts**. Artifacts are things that are used and made by people. One of the artifacts found in the secret room was the Diamond Sutra. This book was made using **block print**. It was made in about 868 A.D. and is one of the oldest known block print books.

The artifacts were studied by **archaeologists** such as Aurel Stein. Stein bought artifacts from Wang Yuanlu for very little money. Stein sent the artifacts he bought to the British Museum in London.

This is one of the larger rooms in the Caves of the Thousand Buddhas. Wang Yuanlu broke through a mural like the ones on these walls to find the secret room.

Today

The Caves of the Thousand Buddhas was made a World Heritage Site in 1987. This means that the caves are protected from further human-made damage. The caves are being protected and studied by Buddhists, scientists, and students from many groups and schools. Some of the groups include the Institute of Dunhuang Studies, the International Dunhuang Project, and the British Museum. These groups learn about the people that made the caves and put together the information to share with the public.

Thousands of people visit the Caves of the Thousand Buddhas every year. After 1,600 years, the caves still help people to find peace and wisdom.

Glossary

archaeologists (ar-kee-AH-luh-jists) Scientist who study how people lived long ago.

artifacts (AR-tih-fakts) Objects created or produced by humans.

balconies (BAL-kuh-neez) Upper floors that stick out part way over another floor.

block print (BLOK PRINT) A type of printing that uses wooden blocks that have letters, words, and images carved into them.

Buddha (BOO-duh) An Indian religious leader who lived from about 563 B.C. to 483 B.C.

Buddhism (BOO-dih-zim) A religion started in India by Buddha.

collapsed (kuh-LAPST) Fell down or caved in.

damage (DAM-ij) To cause harm or injury.

dung (DUNG) Animal waste.

meditate (MEH-dih-tayt) To relax by sitting quietly and emptying your mind of thoughts.

monastery (MAH-nuh-ster-ee) A house where people who have taken religious vows live and work.

murals (MYUR-uhlz) Large pictures painted on a wall or ceiling.

mythical (MITH-ih-kuhl) Having to do with stories that people make up to explain events in nature or in people's history.

plaster (PLAS-ter) A soft mixture of sand or mud and water that hardens as it dries. Plaster may also contain straw or dung.

temple (TEM-pul) A place where special religious ceremonies are held.

warriors (WAR-ee-yurz) People who fight in a war.

Index

A
archaeologists, 21
artifacts, 21

B
block print, 21
British Museum, 21–22
Buddha, 5–6, 10, 17
Buddhism, 9, 10
Buddhists, 10, 22

C
Ch'ien Fo Tung, 9
conglomerate, 13

D
Da River, 5
Dunhuang, China, 5

G
gryphon, 17

I
Institute of Dunhuang
    Studies, 22
International Dunhuang
    Project, 22

M
meditate, 10
murals, 17–18, 21

P
plaster, 14

S
Stein, Aurel, 21

T
temple(s), 5, 10
Ts'un Lo, 5

W
Wang, Yuanlu, 18, 21
World Heritage Site,
    22

Web Sites